Praise for 7

"*7 Days: Manifesting the Life You Want* is a wonderful book, not only filled with inspiration, but insight and concrete exercises on how you can reach the path YOU are meant to be on. It shows you examples of not only the great leaders of the world, but of the common person who rose to greatness, and how we all have our own challenges to overcome. But in the end, if we follow our hearts, we can truly be on this earth and live in joy and abundance through both a spiritual and physical path we were meant to live. Great job, Freda!"

Fran Capo
World's Fastest Talking Female, TV host,
motivational speaker, author, and comedienne.

"*7 Days* stimulates your innate greatness to blossom and become trend setting, as you actively participate in creating a world of joy, peace, and well-being. Freda Chaney's book is inspirational!"

Klaus Heinemann, Ph.D., and Gundi Heinemann, authors, *Orbs, Their Mission and Messages of Hope* (Hay House, 2010.) Klaus Heinemann, Ph.D. is also a physicist and former Stanford professor, author of *Expanding Perception,* and over 60 peer reviewed papers.

Blessings to
Joe & Maria!
love, Freda Chaney
4/29/2019

"What does it take to manifest one's dream life and live in choice, loving the daily process of learning, growing, being, and contributing? Freda Chaney's *7 Days: Manifesting the Life You Want* is a spiritual and practical guide to reinventing yourself, being all you can be and living your best life."

Dr. Joe Rubino
Founder, CenterForPersonalReinvention.com
Creator, TheSelfEsteemBook.com and HighSelfEsteemKids.com

"When I first met Freda at our Empowerment Retreat in New York, she had just driven hundreds of miles with her daughter to be there. It demonstrated her commitment to do whatever it takes to get what she wanted to manifest for her own life. It didn't take lengthy discussions or debates. It was a no brainer for her to attend. Her actions reflected in her book are a testament to taking immediate and massive action to create your own destiny.

There are so many wandering souls who just never take the action to initiate the tipping point and so live life on other peoples' terms and not their own. Freda's positive 'can do' attitude is contagious, and it seems she has mastered manifesting her own destiny from flying a plane to jumping from one. Fearless, wise, and dedicated to positive change, her book will move you, motivate you, and change you."

Carson Tang
President of Powermastery, Division of Carson Worldwide

7 Days

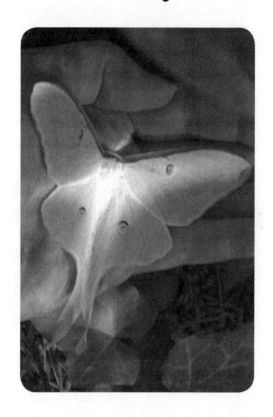

7 Days

Manifesting the Life You Want

A practical guide for learning
how to manifest quickly and easily

Freda M. Chaney, D. D.

BALBOA.
PRESS
A DIVISION OF HAY HOUSE

Balboa Press books may be ordered through booksellers or by contacting:

Balboa Press
A Division of Hay House
1663 Liberty Drive
Bloomington, IN 47403
www.balboapress.com
1-(877) 407-4847

ISBN: 978-1-4525-3854-9 (sc)
ISBN: 978-1-4525-3856-3 (hj)
ISBN: 978-1-4525-3855-6 (e)

Library of Congress Control Number: 2011914855

Cover Design: Freda M. Chaney, D. D.

Because of the dynamic nature of the Internet, any web addresses or links contained in this book may have changed since publication and may no longer be valid. The views expressed in this work are solely those of the author and do not necessarily reflect the views of the publisher, and the publisher hereby disclaims any responsibility for them.

The author of this book does not dispense medical advice or prescribe the use of any technique as a form of treatment for physical, emotional, or medical problems without the advice of a physician, either directly or indirectly. The intent of the author is only to offer information of a general nature to help you in your quest for emotional and spiritual well-being. In the event you use any of the information in this book for yourself, which is your constitutional right, the author and the publisher assume no responsibility for your actions.

Any people depicted in stock imagery provided by Thinkstock are models, and such images are being used for illustrative purposes only.
Certain stock imagery © Thinkstock.

Printed in the United States of America

Balboa Press rev. date: 11-1-2011

CONTENTS

For my family with love:

Norman, Vicki, Todd, Carter and Genevieve.

"When you are afraid of the dark—the
mysterious—the misunderstood,
just remember it was also dark
in your mother's womb."
Freda M. Chaney

Foreword

Life's successes are built on simple principles. Know who you are, go inward, learn how to ask and receive. Through simple exercises that are easy to understand and implement, Freda Chaney takes us on a journey of discovery into our very being to help each of us manifest the life we want to be living.

The key is in having a simple process that you can put to use. The lessons in this book are a great way to put habits into place to manifest quickly and easily. I invite you to discover your own truth, transcend all thoughts of who you think you are and what life could be. Realize that there is a path for you to follow. Gratefully and powerfully focus your thoughts to manifest everything you could need or want in just 7 days a month.

This journey is a challenge, much like the challenge the Luna moth faces in its 7 days of life. Unlike the Luna moth, we each have choices: an infinite number of possibilities and a lifetime to manifest the lives we want. Accept the challenge. Live a life filled with fulfillment and happiness.

Kandee G. Author, radio host for *Nothing But Good News,* star of *The Journey* movie, motivational coach,. mentor, and corporate trainer.

Preface

The cover photo of the Luna Moth begins the *7 Days* journey with its symbolic presence. This mighty green Actias Luna represents intuition and transformation. It lives for only one week after it leaves its cocoon. Its sole purpose is to reproduce. As a matter of fact, it has no mouth with which to eat during its 7 day life span. You might say it lives on challenge alone—the challenge to produce results during that 7 days of its allotted life span. For these reasons, I chose the Luna Moth for the book cover design.

There is yet another reason I chose the Luna Moth as a symbol for *7 Days*. The mighty green moth was sitting in my hand following a rescue. I found it on cold cement, appearing dead. I held it up to admire it, cupping it in my hands for a few minutes. All of a sudden the wings began to vibrate! It lifted from my hand like a Stealth aircraft and flew away into the nearby ferns.

The title of my book, *7 Days*, also has a special meaning. The number 7 is known symbolically as a lucky number. I chose 7 days as my target for using manifestation to recreate my life as I would most enjoy it. The book includes 7 chapters and 7 days of personal workbook pages. While I prefer to manifest during the first 7 days of each month, some are unable to schedule 7 successive days at the beginning of the month. The important thing to remember is to set aside 7 successive days to practice manifestation without interruption if possible. If you manifest 1 or 2 days out of 7 and have to stop, it is probably still more manifesting than you've done in ages! I assure you that once you set aside those 7 days, you will desire that time like a week's vacation every month! It will become a rewarding ritual for you—one that stimulates you to greater endeavors.

With a background in Divinity studies, I have combed both modern texts in the mind/body/spirit genre, and older standard texts for support material for my book. However, this book depends less on others' ideas and more on my own tested methods. As a teacher, writer, and motivational mentor, I've spent years pulling together resources and creating many of my own motivational materials. Moreover, I include written proof of manifestation so that you can see actual examples of how this *7 Days* system really works. Are you ready to create your own world? Let's manifest!

PART I

7 Days:
Manifesting the Life You Want

Chapter 1

Know Who You Are
to Manifest Your Best

You are here to enable the divine purpose of the
universe to unfold. That is how important you are!
—Eckhart Tolle

We are DIVINE! Yes, Divine creatures who can create, manifest, form
something from nothing! Jesus is a prime example. He turned water
into wine at a wedding feast, created an abundance of food for hungry
crowds, manifested 153 fish in a net for his disciples to illustrate the

power of belief. In addition, Jesus brought Lazarus back to life after many days in the sepulcher. He gave sight to the blind, hearing to the deaf, made the lame to walk, and taught that love is the most important key to opening the door—the door that will open if we will only take the initiative to knock.

We are all sons and daughters of DIVINITY! And we create with the same inner Spirit of the DIVINE. In Luke 17:21 (KJV) Jesus told the Pharisees that they should not look with their eyes for the kingdom of heaven.

Another example of a holy and wise man is Buddha. He said, "The way is not in the sky. The way is in the heart." The message, of course, is to look within yourself. Many throughout history have shown us personal Divinity in action, otherwise known as: manifestation, creation, and miracles.

It is written that Buddha instantly tamed an elephant that was about to trample a child. He made tainted water pure, and manifested a bridge in the sky, walking on it for a week! Buddha's list of miracles is long and incredible. Take the time to read about Buddha's and others' miracles of manifestation to help give you a sense of your own Divinity.

The Path

Great philosophers, writers and gurus through the ages have shown us various paths to fulfillment. The first stepping stone on that path is understanding that we are Divine beings—we ARE that path. The life stories of these movers and shakers inspire us because they demonstrate that human transformation IS possible. They reveal to us that we can live on a more compassionate level, not only with others, but also with ourselves.

The great William James believed that personal transformation is what really mattered. The belief in the unseen could, he believed, save one from the pitfalls of life and instill independence and purpose—the ability to rise above circumstances and become great. James himself suffered from depression and used faith to anchor himself.

Mohandas Ghandi wrote in his autobiography that he fought temptations of the flesh and had failed on occasion when he was young. He went on to lead a moral life and by doing so found that he had much more personal power that benefited not only his family, but also others who were within his range of influence. Gandhi led a lifelong search for truth and arrived at his own conclusions about Divinity.

St. Augustine lived a scandalous existence before he began searching for answers about the purpose of life. He found his path to fulfillment and became a father of the Catholic Church.

The well known story of St. Francis of Assisi shares the conversion experience of a son who could no longer exist in his parents' prosperous surroundings knowing that others were without homes and food to eat. Following his conversion, he ministered to the poor and shared Christ's message of love.

There are thousands of written examples of personal transformation. One could write many volumes solely on that subject. The root of these transformations was the knowledge that inside of each man is something more which is unseen by the naked eye—a seed of Divinity. We are each created to be great—to express Divinity in our own way.

Transcendence

Ralph Waldo Emerson grew up in a religious household. It was expected of him to become a minister and spend his life preaching the Gospel in Concord, Massachusetts. However, Emerson could not cope with the fact that his mouth was delivering messages which he, himself, did not believe. He dared to step out of his religious frocks long enough to think about what his purpose was and why.

Emerson initiated the Transcendentalist movement in the 19th century. With a strong emphasis on the individual and the Divinity of man, Emerson's philosophy spread throughout New England and included followers such as: Henry David Thoreau, Bronson Alcott and his daughter Louisa May, Walt Whitman, Emily Dickinson, Margaret Fuller and more. Some may question whether they were all dyed-in-the-wool Transcendentalists, but the fact remains that they were all deeply influenced by the movement. Emerson's philosophy extended to Europe where Fredrich Nietzsche, George Eliot and others embraced his views. Today, Emerson's initiative to explore who he was—to find his individual path to fulfillment—continues to enrich our daily lives.

Whether we agree with a person's transformation or methods thereof, they are, nonetheless, valid for that individual. The important thing to remember for each is that they knew they had a purpose—a reason for making their lives excellent. They knew that inside their suit of skin was a Divine being! Each chose to express that Divinity—share it with the world.

There are many paths—many ways of thinking, experiencing, worshiping and living. It matters not your locale, culture or religion. YOU are the path. Go inward and discover the seed that was planted in your DNA. It is wise to learn how others found their paths, but always make it a priority to find and walk your own path. Then get out there and share what you have learned with others so that they can forge their own paths!

The Inward Journey

How does one begin an inward journey on their own path? Simple—no hocus pocus—just do it. Sit down in a quiet place, close your eyes. Ask your Higher Power, God, the One, your Guide or your Higher Self, whatever you find most comfortable, for guidance. You may first want to pray or surround yourself with white light. These rituals may be comforting to you and allow an easier transition into your revelation of the Divine through meditation.

For this exercise, and future meditations, see yourself as two selves in one: a human self limited to planetary dwelling and the Higher Self who is universal and limitless. The Higher Self encompasses all wisdom and knowledge, and the human planetary self can directly connect with its Divine Higher Self through meditation, prayer and other means. Sometimes this connection can happen spontaneously.

The "Higher Self You" communes with other "Higher Selves." All are connected as ONE. This is probably why we can sometimes perceive others' thoughts or see events in our minds before they happen. We may even be gifted through this connection to other "Higher Selves."

For instance, if you are an artist, and you desire your artwork to be seen and appreciated, you may brainstorm to think of ways to make this happen. Suddenly you have a flash of insight which pushes you forward to become a successful artist who shares artwork capable of inspiring others and assisting them to see with new eyes. This "gift of insight" could very well be from your mastermind group of "Higher Selves" communicating to you those things which you are requesting in earnest. The more enthusiastic you are about receiving, the more you will receive from your mastermind group of Higher Selves or Guides. If our intentions are good, and if we are willing to share with others what we receive, the benevolence of the Universe opens to us on a grand scale.

We Are Energy Beings

We are all energy beings sharing energy wave thoughts and perceptions. Modern science calls it ESP It is by no means "extra" sensory. It is a sense that we all have, but many have failed to use. We must use that awareness to make it as sharp as our other 5 senses. Once we accept that we are all part of one Grand Order of Design—a design of fluctuating energy that communicates across space and time, the world will witness more love and peace. We are all members of one Grand Order of Design.

When you feel fully comfortable within your Grand Order of Design, ask aloud or in your mind, the purpose for your human existence. Then be quiet and listen to every response. Observe every image that flows into your mind. A good time to do this meditation is during the first 7 days when your energy is at peak efficiency. If you find that the first 7 days of the month are not a match for you, then carve out a specific string of 7 days that suits you best.

Remember always to schedule those same days each month so that you have a set schedule for manifestation. The less you confuse the schedule and stick to your plan, the better you will be at manifesting. If you have a schedule, stick to it. Would you call in the President and not show up for the meeting? Why call your Higher Power and not show up for your scheduled 7 days? Having a schedule means you are serious about transforming your life.

Ask and You Will Receive

While you are communing with your Higher Self, you may see in your mind's eye: colors, bright lights, faces, objects, and even words. Your mind may drift to things on your to-do list. Redirect your thoughts to your original question and wait. In the event you cannot receive an answer to the question about your purpose of human existence, try asking a question and then applying a symbol and time limit for the answer.

For example, say you want to know if you should write a book. Agree with your Higher Power that you will see physical proof symbols associated with writing books. In the mind/body/spirit industry these signs are called synchronicity. Set a time limit that is reasonable—say

24 to 48 hours. Watch where your attention goes, and look for the symbols.

Your answer should come easily with symbols of clarification that cannot be denied. Once you have the answer, move forward without hesitation on your objective. Write it down and begin to develop workable goals. Work within your 7 days to accomplish all that is on your goals list for that month. Always make sure the goals lead back to your grand objective.

Guidance from the Universe

I realized this method of time scheduling a response from the Universe works while I was ruminating on what to do with my Divinity degree. For thirty years, I'd been a writer, a poet, and an editor of others' work, so it seemed natural for me to use my writing skills to create self-help and transformational books. But just the same, I wanted to be sure, so I asked the Universe if I was to write a spiritual book specifically about family—my memoirs.

I set the time limit of 24 hours for a response. I used the symbols of books and family as signs of verification. Having done that, I was skeptical that the "experiment" would work. Several hours later while shopping, I sat down to rest and right in front of me on a table was a writing magazine about family ancestry! I needed little more to begin my memoirs, *How Divine*, describing mystical pathways of coping in adult life while allowing the child within to catch-up.

Another personal example I will offer is the moment I felt a strong desire to know if my mother was near and if she knew what I was going through in my life. My mother died when I was just shy of 9 months old, so to say the least, I missed being mothered. I needed to know that her "presence" was still there, though I had long-since adjusted to being without my birth mother. I set a 24 hour time period for the Universe to answer, and I used the peacock as a symbol for an affirmative answer. If I saw an undeniable physical peacock symbol, then my mother was around me and aware. When the 24 hours were nearly over, I was still hopeful but a little concerned that I would not receive my symbol or sign that my mother was around me.

Moments later, I passed a digital clock which displayed numbers I'd long associated with my mother. I shrugged it off as a coincidence and held out for the physical peacock symbol for which I'd asked. Within another few moments, I looked directly at a vase that had peacocks on it. Oddly enough, I'd never noticed the peacocks on that vase until then. I chose the peacock symbol because of the limited likelihood it would be found in our home. When I saw the peacocks on the vase, my eyes widened, and my heart began to pound. I knew this was my answer: first the digital clock numbers, then the peacocks.

I took a picture of the vase and uploaded it into the photo program on my computer. What do you suppose I saw? When the photo was enlarged, I saw a person in a white robe surrounded by children! The person's hair was brown and shoulder length. It could have been my mother, or possibly Jesus, but that didn't matter to me. I'd received my sign through the symbol of the peacock within a 24 hour period!

Peacocks, Peacocks Everywhere

For many days following that experience, I saw peacocks everywhere. My husband took me to a local park where peacocks sometimes roam freely. I decided on the way that I would not capitalize on the peacock symbol since I knew they would be in the park. But the plan changed when we pulled into the parking lot, and I opened my door to find a peacock trying to climb into the passenger's side with me! I had my camera in hand, so I snapped several photos of the peacock attempting to greet me and climb into the van! My husband had to deter the beautiful animal so I could walk into the park. It followed me everywhere I walked and ignored others passing by. We were all amazed.

Another time we visited the same park, and a peacock sat on a bench with me as if to have conversation. Then it moved off of the bench to do a peacock dance in the walkway in front of me. All of this was a truly amazing set of signals to answer my question. This synchronicity—the appearance of signs that clarify direction on a path—had been made truly personal to me because I had initiated the action and had seen it through. So what did I do with this personal information? I shared it: first in my book *How Divine*, and now in my book *7 Days: Manifesting the Life You Want*. My mission began as a method to manifest for myself, but what I manifested and showed gratitude for, multiplied and is blessing others as well.

Manifest Inwardly First

There's a saying that is popular in the metaphysical circles, "As above, so below." Let's expand that thought by saying, "As within, so without." You must manifest inwardly through focused thought and desire before you can manifest outwardly. This is why it is so important to "go within" before beginning to manifest. And once the "thought things" have become "physical things," show gratitude because you have brought into being slower vibrating energy forms for your physical needs. (food, money, car, home) which came from the faster moving energy of thought.

To some, these slower moving energy forms are considered riches. Of course the definition of "riches" is up for debate and is based on the individual desires for her/his life. Most will agree that slower moving forms of energy are best when they keep company with love for humanity—a spiritual base for serving others. Some consider that service to humanity and love are all that matter. We are not here to debate this issue, but rather to bring forth the Divinity of each individual as it lends to the process of manifestation.

Notes to Myself

_____
_____
_____
_____
_____
_____
_____
_____
_____
_____
_____
_____
_____
_____
_____
_____
_____
_____
_____
_____
_____
_____
_____
_____
_____
_____
_____

"You have infinite worth. You are powerful beyond imagination! Once you realize that truth, your world will change, and you will change the world!"
Freda M. Chaney

Chapter 2

Clear Negatives and
Create a Positive Lifestyle

Negativity can only feed on negativity.
—Elisabeth Kubler-Ross

Part 1: Clear Negatives

When I was young, I read a story about a little mouse that loved to dance in a beautiful red outfit. She danced day and night and neglected the necessities. She was so caught-up in dancing and her fancy red outfit that she forgot the rest of the equation that makes life abundant and special. When she realized she was no longer having fun dancing, she looked around herself and found everything was cluttered, dirty and in disarray—just the way she was feeling! She dusted, cleaned and organized her home, and visited with her family. From this experience, she learned that there are preliminary steps to living an abundantly happy life. Little Mouse went back to dancing in her red dress, knowing she had the world by the tail.

Of course, we are each like Little Mouse. We each have our likes and dislikes, our bad habits. It takes standing back and taking a good look at yourself, then being brave enough to make the changes necessary for making your life everything you want it to be. It won't just happen! You must clear the negativity from your mind, body and spirit before you can move on to manifesting the life you want. Here are some options to get you started on your very first 7 days of work—that's right, I said work! Anything worthwhile is worth the commitment to hard work.

The Fun List

First, write a list of what you desire to change about your life (negative mental, physical and spiritual habits.) Next: try one of these tips for clearing negativity. Keep it fun! Make a paper airplane with your list, and send it on its way! Try burning your list together with incense, turning the negatives into a positive sweet smelling savor! Fold your list in half and write on the clean side "DONE WITH THAT!" Better yet, bury it and place a special stone on the site which reads, "RIP, Negative Aspects!" Run your list of negative aspects through a shredder! Post your negative list near the commode and review it just before flushing. (Note: Do not flush the list.)

While these ideas may sound silly, they are methods that just may work for you! A good sense of humor can often be an integral part of the process of accepting change. Andy Dooley uses humor daily as a positive force for change. If you haven't heard of Andy Dooley or experienced his work, go to Youtube and enter his name. Sit back and enjoy!

These actions, together with daily devotion to working on goals, will help you focus on releasing the negativity in your mind, body and spirit. You may think of other ways of releasing negative vibrations such as meditation, visiting a holy site, talking with mentors, reading inspirational and motivational texts and EFT tapping. Whatever works best for you is the right method.

If we could only see what negativity does, we would avoid it at all cost. Continual negativity can lower your self esteem, affect your social life, determine your mental and physical health, decrease your chances of success in your chosen field of endeavor, interfere with loving relationships, halt manifestation blessings, and cause you to see a veiled view of life in general. Negative attracts negative. Misery loves company! The more miserable you are, the more misery you will attract! Get the misery out and the "misery bringers" will flee as well!

Break out of Your Cocoon

Once you have released your negative energy, move away from that cocoon of darkness and spread your wings a bit! Feel the air beneath them as you lift off and manifest your new life—your DIVINELY appointed life.

. . .

Part 2

Create a Positive Lifestyle

Don't Dwell

Wayne Dyer, in his book The Power of Intention, said "If you don't like some of the circumstances of your life, by all means don't think about them." He is correct in his advice because dwelling on negatives that you don't like won't change anything and will even bring more negative circumstances into your energy field. One has to recognize that they can use positive thinking to manifest new circumstances.

Be Gone Negatives!

In my 7 Days method of manifestation, the negatives are brought to the forefront early in the process. They are written down and cleared away so that you can move on to the positive lifestyle you want. This is hard work and 7 days is your beginning—your commitment to the first 7 days of each month for the rest of your life. Some things cannot be cleared easily, and may take a lifetime, but we are hopeful that if you apply yourself, 7 days will become a beautiful ritual that you can depend on time and again.

Our Problems are Internal

Arnold Patent said in his book *You Can Have it All,* "The major obstacle to resolving problems in our lives is that we deal with them as though they are something outside of us. The truth is that every problem is an outward manifestation of our state of consciousness. When our consciousness is clear and at peace, the problem disappears."

So both Dr. Dyer and Dr. Patent are accurate in their assessments that we have to clear our thinking of what makes us unhappy, unsuccessful, unhealthy and all the other maladies that come of negative thinking. The space that is left after the clearing must immediately be filled with positive lifestyle thinking. Nature abhors a vacuum!

What can you do to create a more positive self and lifestyle? Make an assessment of how you are living. How is your lifestyle affecting your daily manifestation? Do you wake-up tired, confused or bored? Are you always feeling overwhelmed? Start with the list below and begin to clear your way to free-flowing manifestation.

Friends or Energy Vampires?

In part I, we talked about "misery bringers" who carry negative energy. They show up where other misery is sure to be found. Who are your friends? Are they complainers—folks who refuse to take personal responsibility? If so, you will become that if you continue to spend time with them. The modern term for such a person is "energy vampire." If you purposely choose to spend time with energy vampires, then you need to ask yourself why. Do you really want to be like them? If they have regular access, you will be initiated and converted!

Check your "friends" list! Surround yourself with positive people, or you won't manifest for the good! Negative friends will try to draw you to places that are undesirable for your positive lifestyle. Just say NO! Seek friends who put motivation, education, healthy lifestyle, and spirituality at the top of their lists. I repeat: you become like those with whom you spend the most time. This truth is vitally important to your well being and success!

Choose mentors who will lift your mood and transport you to a positive place in your mind. Everyone should have at least one mentor and preferably a few in various fields of expertise. If we emulate mentors who are positive, we can conquer our own fears and limitations and become successful. See chapter 5 for more information on mentors.

Gossip Can Be Deadly

Give up the gossip! What goes around comes around. In a work or social setting, gossip is a deadly weapon which can destroy reputations, careers and social statuses, not to mention families and friendships! No one likes a gossiper, so steer clear of them. By following this simple rule, you will be more appreciated by family, friends and colleagues. You will continually attract more positive people into your life who will treat you with the respect you deserve because they will see you as a person of integrity.

Your Environment is ALL Important

Create a positive environment around yourself. Choose colors that enhance your mood. Play soothing and uplifting music. Have a quiet space—a cave to which you can retreat to think and rejuvenate.

I once knew a man whose personality transformed overnight when he changed the color of his wall paint! The predominance of the color red in his environment made him agitated and angry. His counselor advised that he paint his walls blue. He did, and soon he was holding fun parties in his home, and his friends increased incrementally. Note: if you are tired or depressed, red may be the color for you! If you are sad, try yellow and orange!

A Grateful Attitude

Develop a grateful attitude. Always say thank you to those who in some way have made your day better, even if it was a difficult lesson you learned from them. Expressing gratitude is positive and keeps the door open for that positive energy to return to you. Never close doors or burn bridges unless it is absolutely necessary. Stay in touch with those who are an integral part of your growth.

Expand Your Perception Daily

Expand your perception daily. Read, write, spend time discussing those things which enable you to grow and become the best YOU possible. Stay away from things over which you have no control. Actively participate in the transformation of your world by expanding your perception of who you are, and your connections with others of like mind will become evident. They will seemingly appear out of the mists—angels who will help guide you along your path.

Everything in Moderation

Say NO to excessive use of those things which are not good for you: alcohol, tobacco and processed foods! Alcohol and tobacco are proven killers if used in excess. It demands a mention even if it is clearly obvious to most. Some still don't get it!

Alcohol Abuse

Excessive alcohol abuse destroys life in many ways: by causing harm to physical and mental health, threatening jobs and relationships, and taking innocent lives in vehicular accidents. How might the family benefit form the extra cash which is spent lavishly on expensive regular doses of alcohol. I'm not referring to a glass of wine with the evening meal, or the occasional drink or two with friends. There are certain health benefits to having a glass of wine—particularly red wine. Everything in moderation is a good rule to follow, and especially as it applies to alcoholic drinks.

Tobacco Use

It is a scientific fact that second hand smoke can harm those who never lift a cigarette. Many of the baby boomers, myself included, grew up in homes where smoking was the norm for both parents. Unknowingly, they set up their own children for infection and subsequent illnesses during childhood. Many of those same baby boomers are now showing signs of asthma and various cancers as adults. If you smoke, quit! If you live with a smoker, help them quit the habit for both of your sakes. Think of the money you will save on expensive tobacco products. Your friendships will flourish once your best pals don't have to run when you light up! And your breath, hair and clothing will smell fresh again!

Processed Foods

Processed foods can add excess pounds, introduce chemicals into your system and provide little, if any, nutrition. Much of it is not palatable. Food should be healthy, nutritious and enjoyable. The closer to nature you stay, the better off your physical and mental health will be. Eat plenty of fresh fruits and vegetables. If you must eat meat, choose lean cuts like turkey, chicken and fish. Whole grains are an excellent source of fiber. Green tea, juices and water are excellent choices for daily drinks. Buy a juicer and make nutritious vegetable and fruit drinks that look and taste delicious.

You ARE Water

The human body is between 60-70% water! Get in the habit of carrying a container of water with you wherever you go. At work or at home, keep a pitcher of water at your desk to remind you to drink plenty of water during your work day. Water is the carrier for all that is vital to life in our physical planetary systems.

Breathe Deeply

Enough with the shallow breathing! Take in some BIG deep breaths and see how much better you feel! Exercise is one way of improving your breathing. Sitting still and doing deep breathing exercises can refresh you on those days you cannot exercise. Grow oxygen-producing plants in your house and workplace. Ventilate your home often, bringing in fresh air and moving out stale air that may be heavy with chemicals from new construction, interior decorating or household product usage.

Exercise and Family Time

Say NO to habitual TV watching and video games that keep you immobile for long periods of time. Exercise! Get mobile at least 4 times per week. If you are a habitual gamer or TV watcher, you are neglecting physical, social and educational activities that could enrich the quality of your life. Your family ties will be strengthened by choosing to turn off the TV and spending time exercising and playing yard games together.

When you adopt positive habits into your lifestyle, you can expect to reap huge rewards! Your quality of life will improve significantly. Your energy level will go through the roof. You will have less mood swings and a more positive general outlook. Your self confidence will improve with each positive change you make in your lifestyle, helping you to manifest your best quickly and easily.

Preparation for the First 7 Days

Clearing your living space helps free your mind of clutter. Nothing is worse than trying to get started on a work task or writing project only to find that major reorganization must take place before you can begin. At the end of each month, take note of your work area and creativity spaces. Clear out old papers, dust and vacuum, empty trash, re-organize books and files. You will be amazed at what a difference this simple preparation can make in your ability to focus and manifest!

BE READY for the first 7 days of the month by preparing a day or so in advance. Double the positive effects by donating the "stuff" that causes clutter around you to the disadvantaged in your community. Do all that YOU can do, and the Universe will respond to your efforts by meeting you where you are—in the DIVINELY appointed energy vessel called YOU! Like Little Mouse who loved to dance, but learned she couldn't truly enjoy dancing unless her house was clean first, we must "clean" our inner and outer houses so that we can manifest our best. We don't need pills, TV products or fad diets to manifest our best. What we need is a positive, holistic lifestyle change that will transform us inside and out! What a difference we can make in others' lives by transforming our own!

Notes to Myself

_____
_____
_____
_____
_____
_____
_____
_____
_____
_____
_____
_____
_____
_____
_____
_____
_____
_____
_____
_____
_____
_____
_____
_____
_____
_____

"Your style is *your* style.
Define yourself, and let the
world become aware of
you. Set trends, don't
follow them."
Freda M. Chaney

Chapter 3

Enthusiasm is Your Calling Card

"Enthusiasm is the mother of effort, and without it nothing great was ever achieved."
-Ralph Waldo Emerson

Infuse Your Words With Enthusiasm!

As a child, I often visited next door with my best friend and her family. My friend's mother was a rosy-cheeked Bohemian woman who always set my heart at ease with her glowing welcome at the doorway. I visited nearly every day, and still she would act excited and surprised to see me. That did wonders for my little bruised ego. She could have easily turned me away saying they were busy, but she played the part of the enthusiastic angel by allowing me into their home, sharing their love, joy and even meals with me. I remember she announced one day that she'd purchased my favorite candy bars and pointed to the candy jar on the kitchen counter. Her enthusiasm and joy filled my heart and helped me understand more about how my own attitude affected others around me. It was also a great lesson in conditioning myself to have the life I wanted.

All that you say and all that you don't say reveals your level of confidence in your ability to manifest. Your words must be laced with enthusiasm, your voice properly pitched and vibrating with the Universe. If you mumble, curse, or whine, the Universe hears what you say and how you say it, and attempts to match the vibrations. The result will be more of the same: whining, mumbling, and cursing.

If, on the other hand, your words are clear, direct and bold, filled with expectation for that which you have asked or declared, the Universe will match that vibration. The result will be more of the same: enthusiasm bringing forth more enthusiasm around you. At all times, be fully aware that you are creating your own world.

Take Control of Your Own World

Others are co-creating around you too, so your enthusiasm and desire to manifest must be focused fully on your own world and how you intend to live in it. If you fail to focus with enthusiasm on your own creation, the Universe will act on the stronger vibrations of others around you. Your reality will become the product of others' manifestations if you fail to act on your own desires with enthusiasm!

To understand this, just look around and watch how some have great control over their environments—they are leaders. Others have little influence on what happens around them or to them—they are followers. The leaders speak with clarity, state what they need and want with enthusiasm, and typically get it. The followers blend into the energy of others, becoming sycophants who are afraid to voice their own thoughts and opinions.

Energy Vibrations

If we could see vibrations, we could understand this process better. There are fluctuating energy vibrations all around us. If you have ever viewed Kirlean photographs, you know that energy can be seen as fluctuating colored waves. All matter shares this energy in common. Some matter has slower moving energy waves. It is hard to see the energy around a rock since it is vibrating so slowly. But you can see the vibrating energy of a tree in the moonlight if you look just to the right or left of the tree and squint your eyes. That is because the tree is vibrating at a higher speed than the rock. Of course the human body has an extremely high vibration, and can easily be seen in Kirlean photographs. The layers of energy seen in the photographs are called auras. Some can see the human aura with the naked eye, but most can only feel the energy or perceive it.

Your Enthusiasm Beams a Message to the Universe

The more enthusiastic you are, the more confidence you beam to the Universe. The more relaxed and focused you are, the wider and more colorful your aura. Is it any wonder the Universe can find you and distinguish you from others when you are enthusiastically sending out your awesome energy waves of color and movement? Project the image that you want for yourself and you will become that, aided by the Universe with its "like attracts like" matchmaking ability.

We began this chapter discussion with the need to be enthusiastic. Any transformational, self-help, positive thinking or motivational literature will enforce the need for enthusiasm. Zig Ziglar, Norman Vincent Peale, Napoleon Hill, Earl Nightingale and so many others were clear about the necessity of enthusiasm in becoming successful. If all other positive attributes are ingredients for success, then enthusiasm is the electric mixer which brings it all together in perfect form. If you read every self-help book available, you could not *learn* enthusiasm, the calling card for manifestation. You must make a conscious decision to be enthusiastic. Practice with a tape recorder and mirror. Project your voice and always smile while you are talking. During a speaking engagement or interview, smile. Wear a smile even if you are being interviewed by phone. The body can be fooled into a mood, so if you apply a smile and look and sound enthusiastic, before long the brain believes what the body is telling it, and so will the Universe.

When the great miracle workers manifested food for the hungry or healing for the sick, they had to believe enthusiastically for that which they were about to receive. Thoughts are things, but words put power behind the thoughts—project them outward into the Universe. Project with enthusiasm, and don't forget to smile! What you want and need is right before your eyes waiting for you. You just can't see it YET.

Wise Ones Carry the Enthusiasm Calling Card

Disraeli said, "Every production of genius must be the production of enthusiasm." The famous salesman and self-empowerment guru, Zig Ziglar said, "For every sale you miss because you're too enthusiastic, you will miss a hundred because you're not enthusiastic enough." Ralph Waldo Emerson, the phenomenal 19th century philosopher said, "Nothing great was ever achieved without enthusiasm." These historically great men all voiced in their own words that enthusiasm is the calling card to success.

What is success? It is bringing into being a way of life which you desire. How does one do that? One becomes successful by using enthusiasm to spark the power of the mind. While most who read this book are not famous and may have no desire to become so, they can still manifest their best by using the enthusiasm calling card. Strengthen family ties, and enjoy a more abundantly happy love life and social life by being enthusiastic!

Spend time making notes on what sparks your highest enthusiasm, and then act. Manifest while your enthusiasm level is sky high! Write an interview with the Universe, and see how it feels to speak your desires out into the air. Audition for the Universe! Sing and dance, laugh, hum and whistle—anything it takes to get you to an enthusiastic manifestation level. You have the calling card, take it to the door and present it to receive what you desire.

Notes to Myself

"When the conditions are
right, the possibilities for
growth are endless. YOU
are in control
of the conditions."
Freda M. Chaney

Chapter 4

Focus Your Thoughts Like
a Flashlight Beam

Concentrate all your thoughts upon the work at hand. The sun's rays do not burn until brought to a focus.

-Alexander Graham Bell

In the summertime, children spend hours after sunset chasing fireflies. They focus their attention on one thing only: the firefly! That elusive glow kept us mesmerized on the farm where I grew up. We'd swish our Mason jars through the heavy summer skies, aiming deftly at the glowing green angels of the night. Nothing else existed at the moment. That's what true focus is all about.

You must focus to find your way in life, and that goes for everything you do. There are tricks to learning how to focus. Try coming up with some of your own methods. Make it fun by applying symbols such as the flashing fireflies in Mason jars.

Train Your Mind

If you can train your mind to focus like the beam of a flashlight, almost anything is possible. Take out your trusty flashlight and cast a beam into the dark. The area in which the light is concentrated is the area on which you will focus. You have intentionally directed your beam there and not elsewhere. Now intentionally direct your "thought beam" in one direction and no other. Stay focused within that beam.

Negative Effects of Multi-Tasking

The days of multi-tasking are probably here to stay, but to do any one thing to the best of your ability, you'll have to stop being the best multi-tasker and become the best at focusing your attention on ONE thing. Regression? No, progression in the direction you were always meant to go. My grandson is a multi-tasker. Often I have to remind him to "Focus, Hocus Pocus!" Immediately he knows those are the magic words for staying on task one thing at a time.

Objectives and Goals

What is your objective? What is the difference between a goal and an objective? Objectives are: narrow, precise and concrete, while goals are broad, general and abstract. As an example, let's focus on the objective of publishing a specific book for a specific market. Perhaps you have always wanted to be an author, and you don't have a clue where to start.

Use a sheet of paper to list your objective, and the goals that will help you reach that objective. Focus on that big dream, then define the goals that will make that dream come true for you.

Example

OBJECTIVE—I will complete the writing of a fantasy novel within 2 years.

GOALS—I will reach my OBJECTIVE by taking a writing course, I will spend time writing and I will study the book market.

You will find expanded examples of objective and goals worksheets in the back of this book. My first student, Penny, was gracious enough to allow me to provide an abbreviated version of her objective and goals worksheets for my *7 Days* readers.

The First 7 Days-Working on Goals

During the first 7 days of each month, you will work on those goals to make your objective a reality. Always keep your focus on the objective—the dream! For a fun visual reminder, tape a piece of paper to a small flashlight. On it write your objective, then hang the flashlight near your desk for an instant reminder to FOCUS! Focus on your objective. See the sample mentoring session in the back of this book to learn more about objective and goal-setting.

Don't get hung up on the structure of your objective and subsequent goals. It is more important to write down what it is you want to achieve, and keep going back to that list to make sure you are consistently moving forward. Keep it simple, and you won't be daunted by the process. Buy a sturdy 3-ring notebook, and keep your notes in it from month-to-month for a full year. Tracking your progress is the best way to instill confidence in your ability to achieve success on a regular basis.

Manifestation Aids

Create a vision board with pictures of what you are planning to manifest into your life. A Youtube video made from a photo slideshow will serve as a daily reminder to focus on those things or conditions you want to manifest. Record your voice saying the positive things you need to hear to motivate yourself. Your own voice is very convincing when assuring yourself of what you will manifest.

Using these and other "tricks" every day will get you there in good form. You must be consistent in the use of your methods of manifestation. There are no shortcuts to achievement. There are "tricks," but no shortcuts!

Reward Yourself

Treat yourself when you achieve a goal. Buy a new motivational tape or book, take a business success course, get a makeover for the new "successful you" look. Take a vacation or go on an adrenaline adventure!

Let others know about your achievements. It helps to have someone to confirm your progress and assist you in tracking your results. But don't worry if they don't pat you on the back. Change can be difficult for everyone concerned, even when it is good change. Change anyway!

Notes to Myself

_____
_____
_____
_____
_____
_____
_____
_____
_____
_____
_____
_____
_____
_____
_____
_____
_____
_____
_____
_____
_____
_____
_____
_____
_____

"Stop looking for the path.
YOU are the path!"
Freda M. Chaney

Chapter 5

Find Mentors Who Are Vital
To Your Success

Mentoring is a brain to pick, an ear to listen, and a
push in the right direction.

—John Crosby

Mentors

My fourth grade teacher was one of my early mentors. She started
us reading chapter books each day, integrating: art, writing, history,

science and social studies into the reading lessons. I received an award for perfect attendance that school year; that's how enthusiastic I was about my mentor's approach to teaching.

Mentors are vital to your Success. Where do we find mentors? How many do we need? And how long should we stay in touch with mentors? **Napoleon Hill** is perhaps one of the best known motivational mentors in the industry. With his passing, he left an abundance of wisdom in his book *Think and Grow Rich*, which is still being published today. This is a starting point for achievement. Get your hands on the book, or a book on CD. Devote yourself to reviewing the book or listening to the CD daily. I listen to *Think and Grow Rich Instant Motivator* at night as I fall asleep. Earl Nightingale is the narrator of this audio presentation. His melodic voice lulls me into the perfect relaxed state to listen and learn. This rich mentoring from the past reaches into the present like wisdom notes left by a wise ancestor.

There are many mentors who have written books and created programs upon which we rely daily. Some motivational icons in the industry are: **Wayne Dyer, Jack Canfield** and **Bob Proctor**. You can find their work in bookstores around the world. They offer abundant wisdom for your personal application through books, audio and visual presentations, and live workshops and conferences.

Masterful Mentors & Coaches

The following mentors I know personally, and I highly recommend them:

Klaus Heinemann, Ph.D. is an author and respected physicist with whom I am proud to be associated. In 2009, Dr. Heinemann and I joined forces to develop *The Mill on the Floss* project which later appeared in his book, *Orbs: Their Mission and Messages of Hope* (Hay House, 2010) co-authored by his lovely wife, Gundi Heinemann. Dr. Heinemann has been a mentor and ready friend, and his books: *Consciousness or Entropy* and *Expanding Perception* have opened up my world to fresh ideas and concepts. I learned of Klaus via his co-authored book, *The Orb Project* (Beyond Words, 2007) with Miceal Ledwith. Dr. Heinemann is noted for his work with NASA as a materials research scientist, and his tenure as professor at Stanford University. He has over sixty peer reviewed papers to his credit.

Kandee G is the single mom who went from nothing but a jar of peanut butter in her refrigerator to becoming a multi millionairess. She hosts the radio show *Nothing But Good News,* broadcast from a station in Miami and streamed on the internet at 880 AM WZAB, the Biz Radio. I met her in Los Angeles recently at a red carpet event. I'm in awe of her sparkling personality. Kandee is a lady who will listen and remember your name.

Dr. Joe Rubino is the author of 11 self improvement books and several audio programs and films. He has been interviewed on *Modest to Millions, Better Homes and Gardens TV,* and more. A mentor to millions, Dr. Joe is a ready friend and inspirational icon.

Fran Capo holds the title for the "World's Fastest Talking Woman" for which she is listed in *The Guinness Book of World Records.* She is also a comedienne, and world adventurer who has written over a dozen books. Talk about a down to earth friend—this lady is like the girl next door! I enjoy her Youtube video series, *Cuppa Capo.* My favorite book of Fran's is *Adrenaline Adventures!* Get your hands on a copy and learn from a master.

Carson Tang is the founder of Powermastery, the empowerment division of Carson Worldwide. He brought a group of us together in Bear Mountain, New York, teaching us how to bend spoons with our bare hands, eat fire, and walk on broken glass—all to prove that everything really is just mind over matter.

Nik Halik is the author of the best selling book, *The Thrillionaire.* He is an adrenaline adventurer who teaches one to make life an epic, extraordinary adventure. Nik is also an astronaut, mountain climber, wealth strategist, and founder of The Thrillionaires, Financial Freedom Institute, and Sharelord. He is thoroughly inspirational and personable.

Ken Atchity is the author of a dozen books including *Writing Treatments That Sell* and *A Writer's Time*. He is the Chairman of Atchity Entertainment International and has produced over 30 films. Ken is also a top notch professional who assists writers in getting their books published, branded, and made into films. His personable ways and professional manner have earned him a following in New York, Hollywood, and around the globe.

Ridgely Goldsborough is the author of a dozen books including *The Great Ones*. He is best known for his role as host and interviewer on the *Modest to Millions* TV program. He has interviewed over 100 successful business men and women to learn what made them successful. Ridgely is a marvelous speaker and a person on whom you can depend for great guidance.

George Kourounis is a Canadian adventurer, television presenter, storm chaser and explorer. He is best known for his television series *Angry Planet*. George is often featured on: *The History Channel, Discovery Channel, National Geographic Channel,* and *The Weather Channel*. He is very personable, showing up at schools and youth events. He might just ring you up and say he's dropping by on his way to chase a tornado. If you are looking for a mentor who can guide you in adrenaline adventuring, George is your man!

Amy Applebaum is a success, life and business coach and founder of Amy Applebaum, Inc., a company committed to women's success. Amy will work with you on a weekly basis via her coaching program to help you achieve your goals. She is a results-oriented coach and mentor who accepts no excuses! Her rates are reasonable and her monthly fee for the Totally Fabulous Females membership is downright cheap—less than the price it might cost you to buy one meal dining out!

Finding Mentors on Social Networking Sites

How and where can you find personal life mentors to assist you in reaching your objective(s)? Most social networking sites offer incredible networking opportunities with like-minded individuals who can assist you, or who can help find someone who can mentor you. Your mentors must be outstanding in their fields—offering only the best of advice for you to follow.

If you do join a networking site like Facebook, LinkedIn, Twitter, etc., be sure you keep in mind the reason you joined—TO NETWORK FOR YOUR SUCCESS. It is so easy to fritter away an entire day on social networks. Be stingy with your first 7 days of each month.

Finding Mentors In Your Community

Other opportunities to find mentors exist in community groups, churches, learning institutions, businesses and more. Offer to apprentice with a professional in the field or industry in which you plan your success. This is a sure way to learn from the best at close range. Napoleon Hill and many other motivational icons got their start this way. I have been an apprentice in several capacities including an editor and literary scout. I have several mentors, and I'm a mentor myself to students in my *7 Days* sessions. Mentors need not be famous or expensive, they just have to be good at what they do and willing to work with you.

The Mastermind Group

How many mentors do you need? As many as it takes, but not enough to cause confusion! Remember you have to FOCUS! Build a "Mastermind Group" as Napoleon Hill did, bringing the best minds and best advice for success together. This might include a few living mentors and a few icons from the past who have left behind their wisdom in books and recordings. Remain focused on your objective. Do your own thing with their guidance. How long you seek their guidance depends upon your needs and when you feel independent enough to strike out on your own. Some keep in touch with their mentors for many years.

The Right Mentor(s)

Which mentor(s) will be the best one(s) for you? You will find contact information in the back of this book for the recommended mentors mentioned in this chapter. Go online and check out their websites thoroughly before you commit to their programs. They all offer professional mentorship, coaching, and/or tools for success, but their methods and fees may vary.

This is a monumental personal commitment! Take your time, ask many questions, concentrate on finding mentors who match your area of expertise, exude integrity, and are approachable.

Notes to Myself

"Just show up, and you've
instantly set yourself apart
from the masses."
Freda M. Chaney

Chapter 6

Maintain the Power of Passion

> Every civilization is, among other things, an arrangement for domesticating the passions and setting them to do useful work.
>
> **—Aldous Huxley**

Lifetime Passion

I have been passionate about writing since I was a child. I used to close myself into my bedroom and write for hours. Then I would chase down any family member willing to sit and listen as I read my rambling prose and gut-wrenching anti-war poetry. We laugh about it now, but if it had not been for my passion for writing at an early age, I would not be an author today. Writing is a tough business, and if you can't take rejection and hang in there with great perseverance, your passion isn't writing.

This is the kind of passion that is required for true success. What makes you jump out of bed in the morning? What keeps you up late at night? After years of entertaining other ideas, what keeps popping up on the screen of your mind telling you to follow your passion?

A Passion for Lemonade

From a child's first lemonade stand to earning Scout badges, passion is revealed in what we love and spend time doing. Look at your hobbies and it will give you a good clue about your passion, as if you didn't already know.

Anyone in the business of motivation will tell you that passion is a key element to success in any endeavor. The wealthy of the world share this secret. The artist on the street corner planning his first gallery in his mind knows this secret. The mother sitting at her kitchen table creating crafts that she'll sell on the internet knows this secret. We all have a passion for something. We just need to find out what that "something" is and make it a priority in our lives.

The Passion of Steve Jobs (Apple Computer)

In his commencement address at Stanford University, Steve Jobs (Apple Computers) delivered these powerful words to the graduating class. "Sometimes life hits you in the head with a brick. Don't lose faith. I'm convinced that the only thing that kept me going was that I loved what I did. You've got to find what you love." Steve Jobs had been a penniless person before he found that certain passion that catapulted him to fame and riches. Everyone loves a rags-to-riches story, but not all of us are in rags, and perhaps that can be part of the problem. When we are comfortable, we become complacent—just living life day-today without thinking about that passion that is lying dormant within. Necessity, and even desperation, can be part of the success quotient.

Meager Beginnings Give Rise to Creativity

I grew up on a farm where every day was an adventure. We had to make do and find happiness where we could. There was little money, but we never went hungry. As a child, I wandered the woods gathering acorns, wildflowers and unusual leaves. I learned to create with the natural items that cost my family nothing. Soon I had a collection of natural jewelry carved from acorns. I created placemats by ironing leaves into waxed paper and decorating the edges. Collages and dioramas made from items found on a journey into the deep woods, shared space in my bedroom. What was my passion? I wasn't certain then, but I knew I needed to create, and I loved art and writing. I read many books when I was young and began writing at the age of 12. And here I am today, as passionate about writing as I was then.

Solitary Ways

Don't think I didn't take a ribbing from family and friends. Those around me thought I was quite peculiar! My desire to create set me apart from others who preferred to watch TV and play games. I learned to appreciate my own company. Sadly, some never arrive at the conclusion that they need to like their own company, and have to socialize as much as possible to be fulfilled. Socialization is not a bad thing, and in fact in the business world you must socialize to be successful. However, find yourself first. Learn to be alone with YOU. Create your world the way you want it to be. Go within to find what matters most to you—then manifest with passion! Maintain the passionate feeling you had while standing behind your first lemonade stand as a youngster. Wave your hand at passers-by and invite them into your world of passionate creation! Dale Carnegie said, "When fate hands us a lemon, let's try to make a lemonade." I say, "If life gives you lemons, make lemonade and drink deeply. Then sell the surplus with great passion!"

Notes to Myself

"Do you think BIG? If you
don't think BIG, you will
continue to act little."
Freda M. Chaney

Chapter 7

Remember the Mystery of 7

Try not to do too many things at once. Know what you want, the number one thing today and tomorrow. Persevere and get it done.

—George Allen, Sr.

Do the Math

George A Miller, mathematician and psychologist, wrote about the number 7 in an article titled, "The Magical Number Seven, Plus or Minus Two," published in *The Psychological Review* (1956). " . . . what about the magical number seven? What about the seven wonders of the world, the seven seas, the seven deadly sins, the seven daughters of Atlas in the Pleiades, the seven ages of man, the seven levels of hell, the seven primary colors, the seven notes of the musical scale, and the seven days of the week? What about the seven-point rating scale, the seven categories for absolute judgment, the seven objects in the span of attention, and the seven digits in the span of immediate memory? For the present I propose to withhold judgment. Perhaps there is something deep and profound behind all these sevens, something just calling out for us to discover it. But I suspect that it is only a pernicious, Pythagorean coincidence."

The number 7 was considered sacred by all of the ancient cultured nations. It was then, and is now, considered a sacred number in the East. The sacredness of the number 7 spread to the Western continents and is still held as sacred today. Some say the number 7 is a subject of superstition and associated with paganism, but there are hundreds of references to the number 7 within Christian texts to attest to the fact that 7 was and still is a sacred number of Christianity. Our modern use of the number 7 is captured in our music, movies, and in popular books. Daily we find the number 7 a constant companion in following the days of the week to schedule the activities of our lives.

7 Days to Live—The Luna Moth's Plight

As I was planning this book, my initial thought about using the number 7 in my title had nothing to do with luck or the long-standing evidence for the sacredness of the number 7. Rather, it had everything to do with the Luna Moth living for 7 days for the sole purpose of manifesting— producing progeny. In addition, I was utilizing the first 7 days of each month to test my new program for manifestation. That cycle started naturally on January 1, 2010 when I sat down to write out my New Year's resolutions. Here I am 14 months later, with amazing results to prove that 7 really IS a magic, lucky, sacred number! I'm writing this 7th chapter on the mystery of 7 on the 7th day of the month!

I have purposely kept my explanations at a minimum in all 7 chapters of this book. It is short and simple because the real reason for writing this book is to give you the key and allow you to open the door and begin manifesting. Some of you may want to do more research on manifestation and the number 7. I wholeheartedly invite all of you to share your own findings and experiences with me by visiting my website: http://www.7daysmanifestingthelifeyouwant.com.

There are many authors who offer books, articles, audio works and workshops on manifestation, and of course there is a plethora of information on the internet. I encourage you to try my *7 Days* method first, and let me know how it works for you. At the end of the day, the answer is ultimately inside of you. Happy manifesting, and don't forget to use the magic number 7 as often as you can!

Notes to Myself

"Don't bring life down to
your level; climb up to
reach it!"
Freda M. Chaney

Freda flying in a bi-wing Stearman, a dream come true! One of over 80 experiences to date that Freda chose for her bucket list or life accomplishments.

Preflight (in Navy Stearman) photo of Freda in a leather flight jacket and Amelia Earhart style head gear. With her is the owner of the Navy Stearman.

Freda learning to fly their Cessna.
This was her first co-piloting experience in 2010.

Freda's husband, Norman, climbing into the cockpit of their Cessna to
teach her some co-piloting skills. Norman is a private pilot, a professor of
English, and an author.

Freda (right) and her daughter, Vicki, at the Red Carpet Premiere of
The Journey movie in LA, 2010. Another dream come true!

Freda in LA at the Red Carpet Premiere of *The Journey* starring Kandee G.

L-R: My daughter, Vicki Lowery; friend and mentor Ridgely Goldsborough; Freda Chaney; and friend and mentor Nik Halik at the Powermastery Retreat in New York, 2010. We learned how to walk on broken glass, break boards with our bare hands and feet, bend spoons, and eat fire! What fun!

L-R: Freda with her friends and mentors: Fran Capo, world-famous author, adventurer, and "World's Fastest Talking Woman"; Ridgely Goldsborough, author and entrepreneur; and Hubert Lee, entrepreneur.

Freda with friend and mentor, Dr. Ken Atchity, CEO of Atchity Entertainment, Inc., Hollywood, CA. Ken is an author of numerous books including *Writing Treatments that Sell*. He has produced over 30 films including the award-winning documentary, *The Kennedy Detail*.

Freda with friend and mentor, the world-famous storm chaser and adventurer, George Kourounis, director of *The Angry Planet*, and guest star on *National Geographic Channel*, *Weather Channel*, *History Channel*, and *Discovery Channel*.

Freda with friend and mentor, Amy Applebaum, entrepreneur and founder of "Totally Fabulous Females."

Freda with her friend, Val, at Santa Monica Pier, 2010. A dream-come-true tour of LA!

Entrance to Freda's Bed and Breakfast business, her manifested dream come true. The B & B Inn has won 3 national awards for excellence.

"Butterfly on the Angel Column" Freda's photo that appeared in *Angels on Earth* magazine and subsequently on the front cover of *Angels on Earth*'s first daily planner for 2011. The butterfly was a gift from the Universe following the passing of Freda's beloved manor mascot (Pembroke Welsh Corgi) Willie Teacake Chaney.

Freda with her loyal manor mascot (Pembroke Welsh Corgi) Lady Sadie O'Grady, who was at Freda's side during the writing of *7 Days*. Sadie passed away July 24, 2011. Freda created the matching manor capes.

L-R standing: Freda's husband Norm and Freda. L-R seated: Freda's son-in-law Todd holding grandson Carter, and Freda's daughter holding granddaughter, Genevieve. There's nothing like the love of a family to balance all other activities into something truly meaningful for one's life. This is a big dream-come-true for Freda whose mother died when she was a baby.

Part II

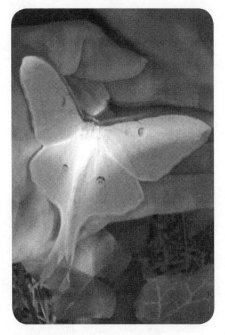

Manifestation
and
Motivation Quotes

by Freda M. Chaney, D.D.

1. Never stop believing in yourself no matter what the world may think of you. The world is not you and cannot be you. Just move along your path unhindered by what seems common opinion—because your life is not common—it is extraordinary and only you can complete the task!

2. Remember the joy and excitement you felt when you were a child? The smallest things could bring the biggest smiles. Meditate on those feelings of joy and bring them back to the present. Use that sensation to boost your energy for manifestation.

3. When the conditions are right, the possibilities for growth are endless. YOU are in control of the conditions!

4. "Balance!" That's all Humpty Dumpty had to say as all the king's men were collecting the scattered fragments of his fragile life.

5. Some say, "Just go with the flow." Whose flow? Create your own!

6. The last word is not written until YOU write it.

7. People with compassion are world changers. Are you compassionate? How will you change the world?

8. If any ONE person had all of the answers to the questions in life, God wouldn't have created so many of us with advice and opinions.

9. Do you find that there are people who fully welcome your praise and admiration, but have none to give in return? That's life; some people are like that. Don't you be *that*. Be BIG. Notice others, give praise where it is due, be supportive and kind, and eventually those things will come back to you.

10. Manifest your best, and leave behind the rest!

11. Wound to scab to scar . . . that's the healing process. The scar is only a trace of the wound. Be sure you don't keep re-imagining the wound! Be the child who proclaims with pride as he points to the scar, "It was nothing really!" then runs into life with full force, living for all its worth!

12. Stuck? Pull your feet out of the mud you've created by standing still and drowning yourself in your own tears. Don't let the giant sucking sound fool you; it is part of the freeing process when you lift your feet and start moving.

13. There is not enough civility in the world. Let's manifest more civility!

14. Expect progress, not perfection.

15. Don't bring life down to your level; climb up to reach it!

16. I'm going to create a masterpiece of this day!!! I AM THE ARTIST in my own world!

17. The camel has something important to tell us, "Always have a back-up plan!"

18. Did you clear anything unnecessary from your space today to make room for something better to enter your life?

19. Your world is YOUR creation. Don't live vi-scare-iously!

20. You write your own story. Make it a fascinating version the world would love to hear.

21. I hear much talk, talk, talk, but when will the WORK begin?

22. Bring your best to any situation, and watch how your opportunities grow!

23. Too busy? Get a life!

24. Imagine yourself on a teeter totter—you on one side—the world on the other. Life is all about give and take to maintain balance. Become a master at balance.

25. Your attitude is a message to the world about your well being.

26. Alignment is essential. Keep on the straight path to your success.

27. In the excitement of creation, don't lose site of the Creator.

28. If the footpaths of others are well-trod and have produced nothing, why follow? Clear a path of your own so that others may follow you!

29. Do not be rattled by what happens around you. Be aware of what happens within you.

30. Do you think BIG? If you don't think BIG, you will continue to act little.

31. Ever feel that a work, social, or family situation is out of your control? Remember you have control of YOU. Carry on and do your best as an individual.

32. Be nice when you are the little guy, and remember to be nice when you become the big guy!

33. Give your customers consistent VALUE, and they'll keep coming back long after new competition has faded into the background.

34. FOCUS: the magic word to the magic world of success.

35. We live in a world of illusions. Don't believe everything that passes before your eyes. Study, become aware, be a student of your own

life and how it will manifest. Don't default to the manifestations of others around you.

36. When you have a question that has never been answered by external means, then the answer is inside of you . . . and always has been.

37. Instead of spending so much time impressing others around you, impress yourself and the rest will come naturally.

38. No other on the face of the planet can do exactly what YOU do. You are unique. Forge the trail.

39. There is one apple that shines brighter—almost seems to beat like a big red heart. Bring that apple into your reality. Climb the ladder one rung at a time until you reach the one apple you're after.

40. If you put all of your apples in one basket, the bottom will eventually fall out!

41. Do you recycle? If you get frustrated with the same conditions or situations day after day, it only makes good sense to do something different. Stop recycling your emotional garbage!

42. Procrastination always takes a back seat!

43. Your life is interesting if YOU are interesting!

44. The brain can be trained—can mirror what you introduce. Your inside world is a reflection of your outside world and vice versa. You are the creator.

45. You don't have to be brilliant to bring forth brilliance. Just follow your desire, focus on the objective, and be consistent. Brilliant!

46. According to scientists who claim they can accurately measure brain function, the average human uses only 10% of his or her brain

capacity. That leaves 90% of the brain's capacity as unexplored frontier. What are we really capable of doing and being? Why not explore and find out!

47. You have infinite worth, and you are powerful beyond imagination. Once you realize that truth, your world will change, and you will change the world.

48. No one can make you do or become anything. Only YOU have that master key. Mentors can lead you to the door—and show you how, but without *your* key, the door will remain forever closed.

49. Don't tarry; some things come but once in a lifetime!

50. It is admirable to look at what's happening in the world of current events and feel empathy for others. At the same time, don't allow it to emotionally cripple you—to stop you in your tracks. What good are you to the world if you are depressed or static? Learn to rise above circumstances for everyone's benefit.

51. Love your family and friends, but always have something "more" to sustain you. Too many of us depend on people to entertain us or bring meaning to our lives. All of that is good, but the individual soul must have something "solely individual" for depth of existence. Find that something solely and souly-individual in yourself and watch manifestation become an everyday event in your life.

52. Stop looking for the path; YOU are the path!

53. Are you SHIFTless? SHIFT happens when you embrace it one day at a time. Don't be scared SHIFTless! Move out there and become!

54. Our world would be much better off if we all chose to remember what we have in common instead of how we are different.

55. I have learned that TIME is very important—not just the time you need for yourself and your own success, but the TIME you need to give to others. The world is dying for a bit of your TIME.

56. Remember a person's name and take time to respond if she or he calls or writes. Learn how to do this as part of your training for success whether familial, business, or socially oriented.

57. It only takes a moment to change a life. Smile and say hello!

58. Every time you experience a small success step forward, you become empowered. Think of each step as a coin in your ultimate empowerment bank. Try to deposit one "coin" daily. Small steps are manageable and will get you there in good form.

59. It's a busy day. Everyone is always busy. Step off of the treadmill for a moment or two and take 3 deep breaths. Close your eyes and see what's under your lids—IMAGINE!

60. Always bring your best and honest self to the table.

61. Life can be rat race. The trick is not to get caught in the trap.

62. Hamster on a wheel? Hop off if you're running and getting nowhere.

63. Be a guiding light for others, and you will never lose your own way.

64. Put what you love first and everything else will follow.

65. Just show up, and you've instantly set yourself apart from the masses.

66. Are you waiting for a written invitation to success? You'll be waiting awhile!

67. When we were toddlers, the hardest part was the first step. Now that we are adults, the hardest part is still the first step.

68. Be genuine! It will shock everyone!

69. Stay in the game even when you can't see the finish line! What's just ahead is always expecting you.

70. Less attitude and more gratitude make the world a better place to live.

71. Think of your life as a pie. Each individual slice is important to the whole. Each slice represents something that makes your life whole and meaningful: good food and water, proper rest, regular exercise, play, work, social life, brain stimulation, spiritual introspection. You create the pie and divide it as you will—holistically.

72. Bend your beliefs enough to include love. You can't go wrong there! You may disagree, but always love.

73. Know, be, and act with the awareness of your own Divinity. Manifestation springs from the root of that knowledge. You have the Divine spirit within you connecting to the Divine spirit beyond your physical self.

74. Be spontaneous with your appreciation of others. The moment is soon lost—and with it the opportunity for good.

75. I used to dream of someday. Now I live each day with wild abandon!

76. For me, excellence is a word that expresses itself when I know I've done my very best. It may not be someone else's mark of excellence, but who cares? Are you in this life to live up to others' expectations? Or are you in this life to become the best YOU that you can be?

77. You're never too old to rock, even if it's in a chair! Rock on!

78. What you delete is just as important as what you save. Be selective about what you choose for your life. YOU are in control.

79. Don't try to impress me with how big you are in the world. Impress me with how big your heart is in the world.

80. Life is full of drama. Refuse to play a part.

81. Growing pains are not just physical. Your mind must grow and expand. Embrace the fear, and the pain becomes a friend that walks with you through life's mysteries.

82. Remember when you were a child, and you played until things were no longer going in your favor? As adults, we can't afford to make such childish moves. Stiff upper lip; we're staying in the game to the finish!

83. Bring yourself fully to the task. Only your full commitment will bring a satisfying finish.

84. Are those around you shocked by your ambitions? Perhaps they need to be shocked out of their complacency.

85. True happiness is created from within first, and the outward signs are the manifestations of those inward creations.

86. How far are you willing to go to live the life you want? Well, here's the good news; the first step is always the hardest, but it isn't far to travel.

87. Want to meet someone exciting? Go inside and find the real YOU. The real you is the brave, exciting one. Break Out!

88. Don't be the caboose, be the engine! When you're the caboose, you only see what's behind you. When you're the engine, you drive the whole operation—wide open wonder into unknown spaces!

89. Plant your fondest dreams in the fertile garden of your creative mind, then watch the miracle YOU grow!

90. What does your heart tell you to do? How does your head try to stop you?

91. You have to go into the mountains before you can cross the desert.

92. The spirit cries out for greatness and yet we stifle it under layers of human weakness. Let's peel off the layers that disguise who we really are—Divinity!

93. When blowing bubbles, you have to blow gently so as not to break them. People are much the same way; speak gently so as not to break the beauty of their spirits.

94. True professionalism doesn't spew and spout. It is considerate, deliberate, and responsible.

95. Life is meant to be lived one day at a time. Make the most of each day!

96. Rock the boat, but know how to swim before you do.

97. When you are afraid of the dark—the mysterious—the misunderstood, just remember it was also dark in your mother's womb.

98. Life is a recipe, but you supply the ingredients.

Freda M. Chaney, D.D.

99. Believing in others begins with your belief in self. The world is a reflection of who you are.

100. To judge someone else is to look into a mirror and curse your own image.

101. Your style is *your* style. Define yourself, and let the world become aware of you. Set trends, don't follow them.

102. If you come in 1st place and don't congratulate those who come in 2nd-5th, you are wallowing in self-importance. If you come in 2nd-5th and you don't congratulate the one who came in 1st, then you are wallowing in self-pity and envy. Either way you lose!

103. Live where you love, and soon you will love where you live.

104. Don't keep your song inside just because there's no visible audience. There's ALWAYS an audience of which you are unaware.

105. Laugh at the things in life you cannot fix, and watch them go away without any help from you! Your attitude is the salve that heals.

106. Express love inwardly and outwardly. It is not selfish to express self love. On the contrary; we don't know truly how to love others unless we first love ourselves.

107. Always keep your face turned to the open door ahead. Stop struggling to re-open a closed door behind you.

108. Just say YES. You never know where it might get you. If you say NO, you've already lost.

109. "But" is a bad word!

110. The word "IF" cancels out every word that follows it. IF you use it often, your life will become null and void.

111. There is genius in every cell, so don't act dumb.

112. Always give the benefit of the doubt. It could be you who is benefiting in the end.

113. The difference between a playground bully and an adult bully is the vocabulary they use to beat people up.

114. A whiner lives with his own complaints long after others have left the room.

115. Is it more important to be RIGHT, or is it more important to be empathetic and loving? Your answer will determine your state of peace and will reach out into the world to affect peace on a global level.

116. If you don't trust yourself—your own ability to succeed, how can you possibly expect others to trust you?

117. A man builds his kingdom from within. Only when his inner kingdom is shared with others, does the outer kingdom reveal itself.

118. Accept your personal power. Understand that it ALL begins with you!

119. Sometimes it takes stepping out of your own shoes to understand what others think and feel in their shoes. Whose shoes are you wearing today, and how might you make a difference in their lives?

120. You have to run faster, be bolder, defy gravity. Don't get stuck in old ruts; burn your way ahead and make your own brand.

121. Greatness begins as a thought. It is up to you to develop that thought to its fullest potential.

122. There is a place in your mind that can make or break you—a place that tells you that you are a winner or loser. Sweep out the dust of past loser thoughts, and usher in the fresh air of winner thoughts!

123. When a person makes and breaks a promise easily, that person had no intention of keeping it. Don't cry because of their broken promise, smile because of your own high level of integrity.

124. What do you have control of right now: the economy, weather, politics, friends' lives, family's actions? No, none of these. What you do have control over is YOU. Your control is not outer, but inner. Command your own vessel, and watch how your world changes from the inside out!

125. Life is supposed to be fun. Remember that when you are planning yours!

126. What we achieve in life begins in the mind—that's the first step.

127. Break bad habits. Refuse to be a slave to anyone or anything!

128. Take the time to know your world. It is a living matrix of energy in which you live and play. Tune in!

129. Procrastination is a thief that will steal your dream.

130. To know yourself is a gift. To know others is sharing your gift.

131. There are dreams beyond your grasp because you do not reach for them.

132. You can't say yes to everything. Be selective in your own best interests. Focus and you will succeed. Be applauded not prodded.

133. If someone else is willing to take their time and energy to believe in you, the very least you can do is take the time and energy to develop that belief in yourself!

134. Map your mission, drive with full focus on your objective, lead with integrity, be guided by passion, arrive safely and sanely at your destination knowing that this is the moment for which you have lived and persevered.

135. Just because you don't hear me complaining, doesn't mean I don't have problems. I'm too busy solving problems to spend time complaining.

136. The difference between being clever and being wise is the depth of the individual.

137. Life has many questions that can't be answered by someone else's truth.

138. Face what frightens you, and be free of it once and for all!

139. Life is full of change. Welcome it! Change—evolution—is GOOD.

140. A loud mouth and obnoxious ways may win the moment, but the real reward is kept for the one who perseveres in patience and kindness.

141. People will call you crazy for doing things they would be frightened to do themselves. Think out of the box anyway, and allow it to move you forward to success.

142. If you are strong and independent, some may never notice when you do need assistance. Learn to ask for what you need. Strong and consistent communication is vitally important to a team's success.

143. Just get moving and allow the momentum to carry you forward. Success requires ACTION on your part!

144. If I told you that you created the life you are living, would you believe me? Good or bad, you did create it with every thought.

145. We dream, create, and excel because we can. No mystery.

146. Receiving is preceded by giving. But giving just to get nullifies the process at the soul level. Give from the heart and gain for the soul.

147. If we had eyes in the back of our heads, we could see what a mess we've left behind. Apparently that is why we have eyes in the front of our heads, so we can only look forward to receiving the best that's ahead of us.

148. Your energy is a beacon to the Universe. It emanates from you and permeates space, arriving at the target destination to which it is sent. Make sure you are sending only good vibes. Your energy is like an echo which returns exactly what you send.

149. Bring it! Bring your whole self to the task, not some half-hearted, wishy-washy, hopeful attitude that does not claim what is rightfully yours. Bring it!

150. Someone said you shouldn't toot your own horn. Why have a horn if you don't toot it?

151. Some spend a lifetime lying to themselves about their limited abilities or lack of talent. Maybe you've said to yourself that you just aren't creative like others. Perhaps you even use others as an

excuse not to try. If you are making excuses, you need to STOP and ask yourself what you fear so much that you lie to yourself and others to avoid trying.

152. Write down this day—mark it because it is of historic significance! Make this the day you realize something new and wonderful about yourself and the world around you! You are the world—the world is you! One—connected. You influence what happens along the chain of reactions. Get busy making a positive difference in you—in the world!

153. Make people feel good about themselves, and they will always remember you.

154. Your dream life is waiting, so what are you waiting for?

155. Get serious about your dream, unless you prefer to joke about it the rest of your life.

156. Even if we could dwell as gods on Mount Olympus, we would not be more qualified to manifest than we are right here and now! We are children of Divinity!

157. What we think, we ARE. Mark it well. We have the master key to unlock the Universe of I AM THAT.

158. Imagine a new you, a new way, a new life. THAT will begin the manifestation process. But it is also up to YOU to bring it fully into the physical state and out of the imaginary state with a little thing called "work!"

159. How many times have you experienced emotional "death" waiting for your big dream to come true? The big question is: what are you waiting for when YOU are the deciding factor in that dream's fruition?

160. Get your head out of your bum! When you are too busy thinking about everyday survival—your bum—you aren't concentrating on the higher "head" aspects of the LEADER inside of you!

161. When I'm tired and don't feel like doing any more, I do more. That has made all the difference.

162. Adopt a "quilt mentality." Ask for help; you can't sew it alone!

163. Entertain thoughts that seem "out of the box" so that your brain has a chance to work on fresh ideas for your future. Otherwise, that gray matter up there is processing information along well-worn paths to the same routinized daily life.

164. Don't pull up roots before harvest time.

165. A good life is one which has your full participation.

166. Change your view of the world—make it benevolent, and your circumstances will follow suit.

167. Create a fresh perspective by exhilarating your senses. Why wade when you can ride the rapids?

168. Invite change! Stimulate your brain by exiting old ruts, and driving out onto the Autobahn of your dreams.

169. Create a brand—the YOU brand. That shouts louder than anything else you have to promote.

170. Get to know yourself, and you will always have a best friend.

171. Be the HEAD and not the TAIL!

172. A joke is only a "joke" if both parties are laughing. Some spend a lifetime having a laugh at others' expense. Publicly ridiculing

others is a type of bullying used to gain notice for oneself. The attempt to make others look small boomerangs and shouts how small the bully really is.

173. The thread of a person's life is woven daily. Choose wisely the colors and textures for your tapestry.

174. According to many physicists, it's been 13.7 billion years since the Big Bang took place. At last, in this day and age of the Super Spiritual Being, it is time for us to SHINE our star stuff!

175. It is easy to be kind to friends. You choose them for your life because they complement you. It is much harder to be kind to family because you have not chosen them—they were chosen for you—the sand in your oyster shell. The true test of love is family. Be kind!

176. Gratitude is Godly, and kind words can pave the way to peace.

177. You are a gift to the world. Be brave enough to reveal the gift that is hidden inside of you.

178. I've determined that some just have a hard time dealing with others' success. Don't apologize for loving what you do and being successful at doing it. That's their problem; don't make it YOURS!

179. Are you a builder or a demolisher? Do you criticize—tear people down, or do you build up their self esteem by pointing out the good things you learn about them? We live in a culture that too quickly criticizes and places blame. Be a builder!

180. Wisdom comes a word at a time—measuring and weighing the possibilities for future.

181. Be selective with whom you let down your hair, or you might just find yourself with some wild chick named Delilah!

182. What have you to do with someone else's attitude? Guard your own castle. Know when to lift the drawbridge to keep out the rats.

183. Break the rules if they need breaking. Go outside the box if the box is too confining. Don't follow a herd heading for a cliff!

184. Fear is the one challenge you must overcome before anything else. It is the monster in your childhood closet that grew into worldwide proportions when you became an adult. If you must, go back and kill the childhood monster, then go out and face the world.

185. If you listen closely to the beating of your own heart, you will hear the beating of all other hearts in unison—we are ONE.

186. Nature is your source. You are the "stuff of the stars!" Get back to your source as often as you can.

187. The beating heart generates more electricity than any other part of your body. Your heart was created to commune with the heavens. Listen up, and love well.

188. Like a cat, focus your eyes on ONE thing. Stay with it until you have what you want. A cat's eyes follow its desire; nothing else exists.

189. Bring yourself to the task—become one with it—master it—and move to the next task. Like knots in a rope, tasks can move us forward to our desired destination. Focus on each one as it appears—that is the key.

190. It is said that if you had a microscope that was powerful enough that you could see into space to the beginning of time. If thoughts are things, could you not also project your thoughts to experience the beginning? And if you can do that, then why can't you project yourself into your YOUniverse and recreate the creation—YOU?

191. If you do one thing with great courage, your life will never be the same. Be courageous!

192. When man learns to master his own inner YOUniverse, his outer universe will also become fully obvious to him.

193. You must fertilize the ground before you plant the crop. You must plant the crop before you expect the harvest. All along the way, add liberal amounts of expectation for the highest good.

194. Quit running around on retreads. Try something new on your road to success.

195. Every once in awhile we need to look into the mirror and ask, "What's your problem?" Come clean with yourself. Honesty is very refreshing!

196. We must do more than dream; we must ACT on our dreams.

197. Not everyone can run around in a pink bunny costume banging a drum, and make customers in the entire world marketplace happy! I'm telling you, it's all about his energy! That bunny has GREAT energy!

198. Remove your garbage before it stinks up your entire house.

199. A quick witted friend is worth a million. A wise friend is worth his weight in gold. An honest friend has inestimable worth. Be honest in your dealings; your integrity is a treasure beyond compare.

200. Tolerance is a big word. It requires a big heart and a huge amount of patience to practice it.

201. Each of you is a pearl of great price, formed in the belly of the world's oyster.

202. A true warrior knows when to put weapons away and love for the sake of love.

203. Expressing gratitude to and for everything frees stuck negative energy! Get it out and get it over with!

204. Positive feelings displace negative feelings. They cannot occupy the same space at the same instant. By expressing positive feelings on a regular basis, you will soon discover that the negative feelings have vanished. They just can't take all that happiness!

205. Gratitude is a positive attitude on steroids directed at everyone and everything!

206. We ALL have great value. No one is more important than another. And should we begin to think our own importance is greater than another, the lessons come to prove otherwise.

207. No one can know the whole truth unless he or she has the capability of seeing from all perspectives at one time. Truth is relative based on our individual belief systems and how we model our lives as a result of those beliefs.

208. Make life your laboratory. Experiment until you discover what works best for YOU!

209. Humans are either insy or outsy—introvert or extrovert. If you are an extrovert, you are probably already displaying your peacock feathers and butterfly wings! If you are an insy, come out

of your chrysalis and show us your wings. Everyone is beautiful in their own way—display!

210. If we don't prejudge, we learn more about human nature and all of its complexities—about ourselves and how we interact as a species. It's as much about an open heart as it is about an open mind.

211. I find that when I give myself permission to say what I really want to say, it always comes from deep within—like dropping a wooden bucket into a well and bringing up pure water. I savor sharing those deep things with those who dare to step outside the busy screenplay of modern life.

212. Practice looking UP where your spirit "wings" are soaring, not DOWN where your feet are trudging in heavy shoes.

213. GET A LIFE! Stop all that moaning and groaning about what you don't have; that's exactly why you DON'T have it! Get busy at being your best.

214. If life throws you a curve ball, get down on its level and slam that sucker out of the park! You're in the game to win!

215. All that you are and all that you do influences the world to greatness or the lack thereof. What legacy will you leave?

216. All guns and no ammo? Before you speak, be sure you can deliver!

217. If you are a cowboy, stay in the fight and die with your boots on. If you are a writer, keep your sources sacred and die with your pen in your hand.

218. Everything worthwhile in life comes at a price. Be willing to pay it.

219. Wing it until you can bring it!

220. Live life fully! Take delight in what delights you, and leave the rest to the undertaker.

221. The millionaire who says in his heart he is undeserving will soon be replaced by the pauper who believes he is! What you believe makes you rich or poor no matter how much money you have.

222. Loyalty is a rare quality in today's marketplace. The supply never quite meets the demand!

223. Life is what YOU make it, so stop complaining and get busy!

224. Everything is not as it seems. As long as you are aware of the illusions, you are unhindered by them in your search for truth.

225. Why bother if your intentions aren't to follow through with what you've started? Don't tease the Universe.

226. Socially acceptable behavior is a must in the professional world. No matter what corner of the globe you are from, there are certain acceptable manners which go without saying when meeting and interacting socially.

227. Life places an immense responsibility upon us. We are on the planet to become the best version of ourselves that we can be. "Just living" is not in the vocabulary of those who take the responsibility of "becoming" seriously.

228. Allow no one to clip your wings! Fly, Angels—fly and spread your blessings across the universe!

229. The Dreamer said, "Dear Universe, I'm writing to ask for my dream life. Can you meet me halfway on this?" The Universe replies, "No halfway here, I'm in it for all it's worth!"

230. Wisdom means being grounded while taking flight.

231. There's a road for serious travelers—the paved one with wide shoulders—safe, nothing new. OR there's the dusty back road, unknown—built for surprises as you go. Off-roading anyone?

232. Give up the struggle. Struggling is the problem, not the solution.

233. The inner self is like a spiritual hand urging the physical hand to reach, touch, and create. Never has there been such intimacy!

234. The only difference between a winner and a loser is the degree of their commitment to excellence.

235. In the end, all that matters is the right ending.

236. Your spirit is resilient even when your body says no. Look up and say yes and make it so!

237. Be the COMEBACK KID! We all make mistakes: some big, some small. What matters is how you bounce back from the walls you hit.

238. Allow no one to clip your wings! Fly, Angels—fly and spread your blessings across the universe

239. Are you living life on YOUR terms, or are you bound by someone else's terms? Bound or free?

240. Look up; there's your TRUE self reaching to lift you out of mediocrity!

241. Launch out and discover yourself. Take no path that speaks of another's going; this is all about you and none about them! Seek your giant within.

242. Peace begins inwardly and moves outwardly to the world.

243. Manifestation begins within and produces physical energy equivalents of what you desire. It is the "work" of the one manifesting to focus on the end result with such a great passion that thoughts (fast moving energy) become things (slower moving energy) for our daily use in this earthly habitat.

244. Good books are like comfy beds: you can't wait to get into one and resent leaving it too soon.

245. Always enjoy your work, and it will never be a JOB.

246. Get a brilliant idea and GO WITH IT! What are you waiting for—a written invitation from the Universe to become successful? Hello, it's out there waiting for you to ASK and ACT!

247. Always have a plan, but allow for spontaneity. Don't get the stitches too tight in your britches!

248. I use 4 letter words! LUCK is a 4 letter word I don't use often. It doesn't involve any action on my part. I much prefer the 4 letter action words like: SEEK, MOVE, WORK, FIND, LOVE, SING, PRAY, TALK....

249. Your words are eternal. Speak wise ones.

250. While someone may suggest a path, only you can walk it.

Appendix A

Acknowledgments

I wish to acknowledge **Dr. Ken Atchity** for being supportive during the early stages of the creation of my *7 Days* program and subsequent book. His pertinent questions and professional reflections helped me come to a decision to write this book.

My respect and gratitude go to **Klaus Heinemann, Ph.D.** who introduced me to his wonderful world of expanding perception. He was gracious enough to write the foreword for my book, *George Eliot Lives*, and has provided an endorsement for *7 Days* as well.

Many thanks to **Kandee G** for writing the marvelous foreword for *7 Days: Manifesting the Life You Want*. Kandee is one of the most positive people I am blessed to know!

I am thankful for **Dr. Joe Rubino**, who took the time out of his very busy schedule to read *7 Days* and write an endorsement. What an inspiration he is to me and to millions of others worldwide!

To the multi-talented **Fran Capo** who endorsed my book and has supported me in ways too numerous to mention. Many thanks to my zany, wonderful friend!

Much gratitude goes to **Carson Tang** of Powermastery who invited me into his world to bend spoons, walk on broken glass, eat fire and break wood planks with my bare feet and hands! I am thankful for the life lessons and for his endorsement of *7 Days*.

I'm indebted to **Nik Halik**, who has been a motivational mentor of mine since 2009. His book, *The Thrillionaire* is a life changer! Nik sets a high standard and lives by it. I am grateful for his friendship and inspiration.

I am grateful for **Ridgely Goldsborough** who believed in me, encouraged me, and pushed me to excel. His book, *The Great Ones* has been an inspiration to me.

To my friend, **Brandon McFarren**, who cheered me on my way each time I shared news about my *7 Days* program. I appreciate his professional manner and efficiency.

My gratitude goes out to **Penny**, my first and incredibly talented student of the *7 Days* mentoring program who made me confident that the program will work for others.

And last, but certainly not least, I want to thank my wonderful **family** who has supported me wholeheartedly in the writing of *7 Days*. Thank you for standing at ringside and cheering me on and for giving up precious moments of togetherness when I had my head absorbed in my writing endeavors. Much love and gratitude to all of you.

7 Days Contributor Photos

Kandee G: Foreword for *7 Days*
(Photo credit: Tracey Tarrant)

**Klaus Heinemann, Ph.D. and wife, Gundi
Heinemann: Endorsement for *7 Days***
(photo credit: Daniel Schmuki, Switzerland)

Dr. Joe Rubino: Endorsement for *7 Days*

Fran Capo: Endorsement for
7 Days (Photo credit: Peter M. Budraitis)

Carson Tang: Endorsement for
7 Days (Photo credit: Jannis M. Turner)

Mentors and Coaches

Kandee G: www.kandeeg.com
Dr. Klaus Heinemann: www.acviews.com/kh/klaus.htm
Dr. Joe Rubino: ww.centerforpersonalreinvention.com
Fran Capo: www.francapo.com
Carson Tang: www.powermastery.com
Dr. Ken Atchity: www.aeionline.com
Nik Halik: www.thethrillionaires.com
George Kourounis: www.georgekourounis.com
Ridgely Goldsborough: www.aviewfromtheridge.com
Amy Applebaum: www.lauraapplebaum.com
Joe Nunziata: www.jnunziata.com
Jack Canfield: www.jackcanfield.com
Bob Proctor: www.bobproctor.com
Wayne Dyer: www.waynedyer.com
Mark Victor Hansen: www.markvictorhansen.com
Anthony "Tony" Robbins: www.anthonyrobbins.com
Rollan Roberts II: www.idream247.com
Jim Rohn: www.jimrohn.com
Brian Tracy: www.briantracy.com
Steven Covey: www.stevencovey.com
T. Harv Eker: www.harveker.com
Dave Ramsey: www.daveramsey.com
Jordan Goodman: www.jordongoodman.com

Appendix B

7 Days of Manifestation Sample

May 1-7, 2010

Books—the Yes and No of It:

On May 1, 2010, my husband and I visited a local bookstore where I searched a bookshelf that contained a number of George Eliot books by Signet and Oxford—the common ones you can buy anywhere. Disappointed, I asked the Universe to manifest the George Eliot book that would be most beneficial to me in my research. Looking again, I found the very book I'd hoped for in that store full of overstock and discontinued books. It was the improbable gem in the mine, and there it was on the same shelf where I'd previously searched!

Earlier that day, I sat at breakfast and told my husband of a title for a book which popped into my head. I had been wanting to write a book about natural facelifts. The title I thought of was *Forget The Facelift*. That day, we went to a bookstore to peruse the titles to see what was published on the subject of facelifts. Guess what? The book *Forget the Facelift* was already published, and it was sitting in a clearance bin! I had manifested proof NOT to write the book, but to move in another direction. This is when I decided the Universe was looking out for me and not just sending me stuff! It made NO as clear as YES.

That same day, I had the thought in my mind to collect *Tintin* comic books. We were ready to leave the bookstore when I felt a prompting, "You must at least ASK." My husband was already checking out with an armload of books, but I asked him to wait. I paced back to the information desk and asked about *Tintin* comic books. The assistant looked at his computer for about a minute and then said, "There's one." He walked me back to the bookshelf where *Tintin* was supposed to be. It was not there. The assistant scanned the shelf twice. He said there could be two more places the book might be shelved. He walked away.

When he returned he was baffled, saying it was not in back and it was not on the "other" shelf. All of the sudden I *knew* there was a *Tintin* book on the top shelf where the assistant had looked twice. I said, "Are you sure you scanned that top shelf well? I can't see that high, but I feel the book is up there!" He said he was sure he'd looked well, but he would look again. His jaw dropped when he saw not one, but three *Tintin* comic books on that top shelf! He said, "I'm confused; there's only one in the computer system! And I scanned that shelf twice!"

I believe one of the keys for manifesting books is my stated intention of earning a living writing. I have helped others with their writing before I began working on my own books. Last year, I edited 3 books for free; one was actually ghost-written by me. I also edited stories and submitted them to magazines for others to give them a start. I have learned that what you give, you receive back from the Universe. There is plenty to go around. This is a concept that many don't understand—the law of reciprocity.

Money:

On May 4, 2010, I looked over my business budget and found I was $495.00 deficit for the upcoming month, so I determined to manifest the necessary funds. I focused on my objective by seeing $495.00 in my mind. In addition to my visualization of the numbers $495.00, I saw a telephone. I went to the telephone to see if I had missed any messages for B & B lodging prospects on the answering machine. None. I couldn't just walk away and dismiss the thought, so I looked at the calls from the previous days on the caller ID. There had been a call logged from the day before. It felt "lucky" so I called the number. An answering machine picked up my call on the other end. I left a message saying I'd seen the number on the caller ID and was just checking to see if they needed lodging. I hung up the phone wondering why I had done such a thing. In the twelve years of managing my B & B, I had never called a Caller ID number back, only responded to direct calls, answering machine messages and online queries.

The next day there was a phone call from the person whose number I'd found on the Caller ID. Guess what? She reserved the last suite available for a local event for 3 days—the exact amount $495.00!

A few days later, but still within the first *7 Days* timeframe, I manifested money the exact same way. I looked at the caller ID and visualized $250.00. I saw a number that appeared to be a residence, and called it. When a man answered, he was surprised I'd called even though he'd not left a message. I told him I was calling as a courtesy. He said they needed a room for two days. I charged $125.00 per day, so his total came to $250.00 before taxes!

While these are not huge sums of money, it is a beginning of understanding that money is energy just like everything else, and it can be manifested.

Relationships:

The *7 Days* method also works with relationships. In April 2010, a friend of mine sent a negative e-mail and went on disconnect with me. I thought I'd let her ride it out hoping she would get over it. Two weeks passed, but she had not corresponded. On May 1st, I took that negative e-mail she had written, folded it, wrote "LOVE" on it and placed it on my desk in plain view. I sent love to the Universe every time I looked at the word "LOVE" on that e-mail. Soon my friend wrote to express appreciation for a check that had just arrived from the publisher to whom I'd submitted her work. *7 Days* works for others by blessing them through steps you take for them. Imagine how the *7 Days* method would work for family relationships, for co-workers, and for friends!

How Does it Work:

I made the intention on January 1, 2010 to re-create my world during the first 7 days of each month during the year 2010. The Universe is cooperating with me, and particularly because I am tuned in on those scheduled seven days. That's not to say I don't work hard on other days, or that I don't earn money during other days of the month, but it does mean that on the days 1-7, everything is accelerated around me as though the Universe has agreed to cooperate during those times if I will agree to be there and receive. Remember the Fatima and Lourdes miracles? The children were instructed to return on a set date. They agreed, and the apparition appeared with miracles following. A schedule followed for the "miracles" to occur. In my case, it would seem I'm setting my own schedule, unless the Universe placed the initial idea into my head to manifest on the first 7 days of the month.

Thoughts are things—I reach out and work them as though they are real, and they are! Visualizations in your mind are as real as the things you can touch. Set your intentions, visualize the outcome, set a timeline, move immediately to "create" the result. Don't sit there and expect it all to come to you without effort.

When something is manifested, record the results and tell someone in writing so you will have a witness of the event, time, date, location. Even if you have some doubts, just keep moving forward.

And last, but certainly not least, share what you manifest to keep the energy moving and blessing others. Eventually, it will circle back to bless you again and again.

Appendix C

Sample *7 Days* Coaching & Mentoring Session

My first *7 Days* mentee, Penny, graciously agreed to share her mentoring session worksheets with my readers. The following information was a follow-up to an introduction session. We talked about her objective, and a few subsequent goals. Following each regular session, Penny and I spent time in a question and answer period. I have not included those private sessions. Penny is a fictitious name to protect the interests of the participant.

Penny's *7 Days* Sessions:

OBJECTIVE:

Within _____ months, Penny will be using her music degree in a professional way, earning approximately $_____per year.

GOAL 1: Find Work Using Your Music Degree

1   Join social sites to enhance your networking capability:

A Join Linkedin http://www.linkedin.com/ Join groups of interest once your bio is complete.

B Join Twitter: http://twitter.com/ Choose your Tweet companions to enhance your career.

May I also suggest you look into being listed in professional directories and seek membership in organizations associated with the music industry. Here's a link that has a lot to offer: http://dir.yahoo.com/entertainment/music/organizations/

Expanded Goals (Suggestions):

2 Create professional hand outs to promote yourself:
   A Current biography in Word format with professional photo inserted, include references.
   B Current professional photo
   C Business cards with photo insert (worth the investment in the long run)
   D Color flyer of basic contact information, skills and photo for inclusion in intro package.
   (This can be created with a good photo program which we will discuss on day #2.)

3 Contact local businesses and services to promote your career:
   A Wedding planners
   B Check with Visitors Bureau for local venues for entertainers

4 Set up a home-based business:
   A Teach music lessons from home
      1. Piano lessons
      2. Singing lessons

5 Opt for print advertising:
   A Local papers
   B Marketing inserts

C   Yellow Pages
D   Church bulletins
E   School promotional directories

End of Day 1 of Penny's *7 Days* Mentoring Sessions

Testimonial from Penny

"This was actually my first ever mentoring program. Before this program, I thought that I knew all there was to manifesting, even though I had received very little of what I wanted. Freda takes the mystery and "magic" out of manifesting and makes it very simple, straight forward, and so easy! She made things that seemed so far away and distant, and maybe even impossible to reach more attainable and very realistic. She has such a great gift of making whatever you're reaching for so real and down to Earth. I definitely recommend her program to anyone who needs a little extra push in the right direction. Thank you, Freda for such a wonderful mentoring experience!" . . . Penny

Note from Author:

I am very proud to report that within a few short weeks Penny began a major transition in her life to advance her career and promote her talent. She is recording her original songs and posting them for public comment on Youtube. She has learned the power of focusing on what she really wants for her life and is taking action on it immediately.

Appendix D

Resources for *7 Days*

Enjoy my Youtube videos designed to assist with the process of manifestation. Please note that my Manifestation Movie is a "mind movie" designed to assist the listener in manifesting all the best for her or his life. The scenes and thoughts shared in the video are simply suggestions for manifestations and prosperity. The house and car in the Youtube "Manifestation Movie" below are not mine, but rather models used for illustrative purposes only. You can create your own "mind movies." Select photos of the life you would like to manifest, add appropriate captions, upload to Youtube and apply music. It's easy once you get the hang of it. Now go out there and manifest YOUR best!

Links for Freda's Videos and Websites:

http://www.7daysmanifestingthelifeyouwant.com/ Enjoy my official *7 Days* book website.

http://www.youtube.com/watch?v=9NvNjU08Z-M
Enjoy my free *7 Days* "Manifestation Movie" video tool to enhance your visualization of the things you desire for your own life.

http://www.youtube.com/watch?v=AXmZTw8HlM0 Enjoy my free "Prosperity Blessing" video tool for blessing yourself and others.

http://www.youtube.com/watch?v=z5byi_VLGPk Enjoy my free "Walking at the Waterfall" meditation video tool for relaxation and visualization.

http://www.youtube.com/watch?v=C4wGk_X_XGk Enjoy my free first flight as co-pilot experience "The Greater Lessons of Flying" to help manifest and apply your best.

"If the footpaths of others are well
trod and have produced nothing,
why follow? Clear a path of your
own so that others may
follow you."
Freda M. Chaney

About the Author

Freda M. Chaney wears many hats as an author, literary scout, entrepreneur and administrator of several motivational websites. She attended Otterbein College and earned a doctorate degree in Divinity through American Institute of Holistic Theology. Her writing career spans thirty years, and includes: books, magazine articles, and award-winning poetry. Freda is the wife of Professor Norman Chaney, mother of artist Vicki Lowery, and proud grandmother of Carter and Genevieve.

In 2009, Freda had the honor of working with physicist and co-author of *The Orb Project* (Beyond Words), Klaus Heinemann, Ph.D., and his wife Gundi on their recent mind/body/spirit book *Orbs: Their Mission and Messages of Hope* (Hay House 2010.) Freda's book *George Eliot Lives* is a full account of the story that appears in the Heinemann's book.

In 2010, Freda had the honor of sharing her ideas and notes for her book, *7 Days: Manifesting the Life You Want*, with her friend, Dr. Kenneth Atchity, an author and producer in Hollywood. Dr. Atchity mentored Freda through the process of pulling her notes together for her book.

Freda Chaney is a supporting member of The Institute of Noetic Sciences. She shares manifestation and inspirational thoughts daily on her book websites and on social sites and blogs. Freda has been a local keynote speaker and is listed in *Marquis Who's Who* publications.

Manifesting and recording the information for *7 Days* took one full year. It is Freda's sincere desire to share this simplified method of manifestation with others through her book, videos and other support materials. See the "Shop" page on the official *7 Days: Manifesting the Life You Want* website. Go to: http://www.7daysmanifestingthelifeyouwant.com

33437008R00085

Made in the USA
Lexington, KY
11 March 2019